Phonics Focus: sound of au

THE LAUNCH

BY CHRISTINA EARLEY

**ILLUSTRATED BY
ANASTASIA KLECKNER**

A Blue Marlin Book

SEAHORSE
PUBLISHING

Introduction:

Phonics is the relationship between letters and sounds. It is the foundation for reading words, or decoding. A phonogram is a letter or group of letters that represents a sound. Students who practice phonics and sight words become fluent word readers. Having word fluency allows students to build their comprehension skills and become skilled and confident readers.

Activities:

BEFORE READING

Use your finger to underline the key phonogram in each word in the *Words to Read* list on page 3. Then, read the word. For longer words, look for ways to break the word into smaller parts (double letters, word I know, ending, etc.).

DURING READING

Use sticky notes to annotate for understanding. Write questions, make connections, summarize each page after it is read, or draw an emoji that describes how you felt about different parts.

AFTER READING

Share and discuss your sticky notes with an adult or peer who also read the story.

Words to Read:

auks	August	sauna
haul	auto	astronauts
lauds	Autumn	audience
sauce	bauble	audio
fault	daughter	autograph
jaunt	launching	nautical
launch	pauses	sausages
applauds	saucy	

"Let's go watch the spaceship launch," Autumn says.

"Great idea, daughter!" August says. "I will drive our auto."

The audience looks toward the launching pad.

The countdown clock pauses. Why? It is the fault of a flock of auks!

8

The audio counts down the last seconds: 10...9...8...7...6...5...4...3...2...1!

The spaceship lifts off. It carries astronauts into the sky.

The audience applauds!

The fire from the boosters feels as hot as a sauna.

"Let's get something to eat at the Saucy Dogs food truck," says Autumn.

"Two sausages with mustard sauce, please," August orders.

They haul their lunch to a table.

An astronaut gives Autumn an autograph and a bauble.

"That was a fun jaunt," Autumn lauds. "Next, let's do something nautical!"

AUTOGRAPHS

13

Quiz:

1. True or false? Birds stop the launch.
2. True or false? August is Autumn's mother.
3. True or false? August and Autumn have hamburgers for lunch.
4. Why do you think an astronaut gave an autograph and a bauble to Autumn?
5. What is the genre of this book? How do you know?

Flip the book around for answers!

Activities:

1. Write a story about Autumn and August's nautical-themed day.

2. Write a new story using some or all of the "au" words from this book.

3. Create a vocabulary word map for a word that was new to you. Write the word in the middle of a paper. Surround it with a definition, illustration, sentence, and other words related to the vocabulary word.

4. Make a song to help others learn the special sound of "au."

5. Design a game to practice reading and spelling words with "au."

Written by: Christina Earley
Illustrated by: Anastasia Kleckner
Design by: Rhea Magaro-Wallace
Editor: Kim Thompson
Educational Consultant: Marie Lemke, M.Ed.
Series Development: James Earley

Library of Congress PCN Data
The Launch (au) / Christina Earley
Blue Marlin Readers
ISBN 978-1-6389-7997-5 (hard cover)
ISBN 979-8-8873-5056-1 (paperback)
ISBN 979-8-8873-5115-5 (EPUB)
ISBN 979-8-8873-5174-2 (eBook)
Library of Congress Control Number: 2022944993

Printed in the United States of America.

Seahorse Publishing Company

seahorsepub.com

Published in the United States
Seahorse Publishing
PO Box 771325
Coral Springs, FL 33077